NEW NUMBERS

The New Issues Press Poetry Series

The New Issues Press Poetry Series is sponsored by The College of Arts and Sciences, Western Michigan University, Kalamazoo, Michigan

An Inland Seas Poetry Book

Inland Seas poetry books are supported by a grant from The Michigan Council for Arts and Cultural Affairs.

Printed in the United States of America.

First Edition, 2000.

ISBN: 0-932826-93-8 (paperbound)

Library of Congress Cataloging-in-Publication Data:
Kearns, Josie
New Numbers/ Josie Kearns
Library of Congress Catalog Card Number (99-076772)

Art Direction:	Tricia Hennessy
Design:	Donna Dickmann
Production:	Paul Sizer The Design Center, Department of Art College of Fine Arts Western Michigan University
Printing:	Courier Corporation

NEW NUMBERS

JOSIE KEARNS

New Issues Press

WESTERN MICHIGAN UNIVERSITY

This book is dedicated
to Joseph Matuzak
for his patience and inspiration.

Contents

Acknowledgements

Thanks to the editors of the following journals in whose pages these poems first appeared, often in earlier versions:

Poetry Northwest: "New Numbers," "Sping," "Quaro," "Leethum," "Thyr," "Hystra," "Eenum," "Callarum," "Kisura," "Xelah Xalong," "Philium."

The Bridge: "Cehu."

Many of the New Numbers poems were in a chapbook published by March Street Press.

These poems were written with the help of grants from the Michigan Council for the Arts and Cultural Affairs (now Artserve). Several of the New Numbers poems were awarded the first MacLeod-Grobe Prize from *Poetry Northwest*.

The author wishes to thank the Avery Hopwood and Jules Hopwood Foundation, the Cowden Fellowship Committee, and especially the contributors and staff at Ragdale Foundation, the writer/artist colony in Lake Forest, Illinois without whom these poems might never have been finished.

The author also wishes to thank Richard Tillinghast, Alice Fulton, Thomas Lynch, Tom Lux, David Wagoner and David Sosnowski who read versions of these poems; and teachers and friends too numerous to mention individually.

New Numbers

"We need new numbers for this."
Scientist explaining the term 'overkill' to Congress.

Because we can't keep count of the daily murders.
Because 12583 dead doesn't mean anything.
Because every 5 minutes immeasurable harm happens.
Because of 1 in 10 and 4 out of 5.
Because 22% think the Holocaust didn't happen.

Because we escape time through the doorway of digital exactness.
Because the National Park Service says 300,000 and the marchers
say 1.2 million.
Because we tally the exact spasms of a man's body
in the electric chair and his name is 789632556.

Because humans are branded with them.
Because the likelihood of a teenager having an abortion is 1 in 5
and the likelihood of telling her father is zero.
Because 5,832 nuclear installations must be wrong.
Because graves outnumber affordable housing 25,000 to 1.
Because the 21st century must be redefined.

Because it is possible for every voice
And every word of every voice
And every letter of every word of every voice
And every part of every letter of every word of every voice
to pass into nothingness.

Continuum Number

My mother is writing a poem.
She doesn't use the words I would.

It has things in it like Cloverine
Salve and something about
a red-headed woman named Venus.
There's a lot about coal.
And coal shoveling, breaking up a chair
for heat. About winter in 1954
late March, when she and this
Venus fooled brooders? No, boarders,
about the lack of heat. Nothing
yet about me.

But currently, about my older sister
how she was afraid of the dark
bituminous chute (I never knew that)
and how the next oldest sister hated
waiting for the iceman, wait, she scratched
that out, feared that the food in the icebox
was decaying, rotting away like
her wisdom tooth. This was before
they used nitrous, my mother notes.

Much later, there's a little something
about me, but the letters fade in the low light.
Why does she write under such low light?
After all, she always told us, reading
Batman comics by the hall bulb,
"Do you want glasses like mine?" That
part isn't in there, but something about me
throwing coal, big, cokey chunks, at a boy,
Leonard Zwicker, one evening, and ruining

her hand at gin rummy. Then a recipe.
Rhubarb pie. The stanza ends there.
Why is there so much about coal?
Where's more about me?

Sping

Is the straw
and the camel and its back
and the last haystack in which
the poison needle is found.

Sping is the exact number of times it will take
until the small, aging man snaps
the haranguing wife, boss, friend, lover
finds the hatchet, tire iron, hammer, blade.
How the kerosene, torch are located.

How Rosa Parks found her bus seat.
Sping is the dustbowl and Black Tuesday.
Sping is the dodo and passenger pigeon packing up.
How the child was found in the well.
Sping is the Code of Hammurabi and the Fifth Amendment.
Sping cannot always be trusted.

Sping = x when x is why?
Sping is greater than city hall.
Sping is why waves and wherefores break
        the waves mounting into revolution arguments
        the shore receding until Ushers fall
        the critical mass of starlings, the breakpoint
        of white tigers, the avalanche of the zebra mussel
                the zeitgeist of
                        pterodactyls and monsoon winds

all begin with Sping.

This tiny prime cannot be divided.
"I just couldn't take it anymore."
It is the personal number of those put aside
        putting aside, putting aside

a binomial in the formula
of real and imagined victims and

it is enough.

Clazura

In the fishing tackle box
Ed, the ex-boyfriend, bought me
Ed, who smoked Marlboros
while filling the boat's tank with gasoline

yelling at me to watch
for sandbars and drowned tree limbs
while snow fell on the Au Sable River
soft as the lovemaking we would never return to

and the DNR boys, nabbing
salmon snaggers like flies
shaking their heads at us
from the far off shore.

In the fishing tackle box
are hooks twisted as serial killers
the fate of three bass, two trout, six perch
one sunfish

silver-hooked sirens
in white and black gowns
waving out like Chinese fans

orange and green speckled slithers
wriggling their allure
five, ten, fifteen, twenty-five lead weights
like silent diving bells
pewter and solemn

snapped, heroic lines
snarled reels
red and white floats
bobbing like messengers between worlds

the guts of two worms
transparent filaments of fish line
like the trail of comets or planes.

Quaro

is the number beyond knowing.
Out there in the Milky Way on the event horizon
of an infinite continuum.

Quaro is the thoughts in the universe.
Quaro redefines pi.
Quaro is not for everyone.

As unknowable as souls.
As uncontrived as gravity.
Quaro is the number of times you will be
remembered after you die
and the number of your rebirths.
It is said:
Not even the moon knows quaro.

"Quaro," a mother says.
But not yours, this mother in the future
where quaro is discussed as commonly
as how rain forests regenerate
through a thousand years of peace.

That mother says to her child
"If you knew quaro
the pinata of sky
would open up
and break down all the stars for you."

Endearth

There's never any more cold like that
freezing so much you don't dare move quickly.
But inside, steam rises like hope in your childhood
breast. Hope for seconds and a break from first

hour math. Her idea was to make us a hot breakfast
since she worked, making up for time away.
There were pancakes even. Syrup dribbled around.
I remember I wanted to put some in my boots.

And the scrambled eggs, like yellow clouds of rain
along the Yangtze Shuko would tell me about in college.
I would never go there. And the toast had real butter,
melting in excess like a mudslide in April. All the food

was coming down my stomach like that, too much, fast.
Awake at 6:15 a.m. an hour before the ride came, I was
becoming a memory in my own life. I was getting closer
to forty and her death, and when the Buick would honk,

scoop us away and we'd be done with all her work. But
the diced potatoes took the longest to prepare, so, waiting
for their sizzle, she squeezed orange juice, told us, "Drink
it before the vitamins escape!" So I had this vision: C and B12

jumping out of my glass like our goldfish did once. There was
fancy ketchup like sorbet for the meal. But the diced potatoes,
perfectly browned even black on some sides,
    uniform masonry blocks,
salty, as if each side told something different
    about us besides failure.

Eenum

This is the number we mean
when we say, “one, two . . . many.”
Palms and fingers spreading out
like amazed umbrellas sheltering the knowledge:
lives lost on the battlefields
and the battlefields.
The stitches of violence and time.

Eenum tallies the bills and overdue notices
auto repairers and lawyers
cheating: eenum.
Your blood pressure is eenum.
Government mistakes are eenum.
Eenum is counting the fortunes
of someone else against your own—
how you were passed over, lost out
missed essential connections: eenum.

Eenum is accepted apologies between lovers
the excess of every century, even the seven lean years
          even in Ethiopia, Appalachia, Bangladesh, Harlem
          where it is a kind of howl, howling in excess
          where the eenum and the few dance with
          their partners of “hold fast” and “next time around.”

This is eenum:
your own dreams in the darkness
you will never remember
and their warnings coming true.

Hystra

Choosing the day I'd live over is simple:
my mother's 39th birthday
when I rode my Schwinn like a schooner
down cracks of breakneck driveways,

This is the placeholder:
The cache of souls unopened,
Bernadette's letter sealed.

Six streets over to the Ben Franklin's
to buy with my own dollar the thin, glass-blown
chalices, one-use-only, "Fragrances of the World":

An isotope zero
where your fused and unfused life
becomes matrix.

Evening in Paris, Tigress, Ambush, Tabu
titles as dangerous as the 7-Up and chablis mix
she sometimes let me sip at parties.

A continuum of ladder and hinge:
what swings there
not even the moon
knows the end of

where mounds of potato salad and rhubarb pie
and the blueberry cake Aunt Ann baked that day
would greet her with my step-father, Ray's, gift
of the double-sink kitchen cabinets when we shouted

as a plutonium zero
as a cascade
woven by the dead

"Surprise!" and her loam brown eyes
misted over and I was still
nine or ten

like a pressure valve
an airlock wheel
on a submarine

And the cards of canasta and gin rummy
the Old Grandad whiskey bottle, never empty
(by which I mean Ray did not drink
like my father)

The last Chinese box
in the long tradition of boxes.
The door that is a box.

my brother-in-law and step-father sitting
at the yellow and chrome kitchen table
and the lumber soon to be painted
"redwood" stacked outside like bonds
to ensure a future of perfect fences

1066
November 22, 1963
Cinque de Mayo
2001

where it fell to these men, white
t-shirted and overalled, to pound in the poles
of that fence as if this life would stay
where we put it.

the Secret Annex
never found

And I fell
asleep that night under
that same table listening to the grinding
of stories my aunts told, voices
lifting me toward sleep

our private compartment
your false wall, hidden spring
survival kit

in a language as foreign and majestic
as Lima, Peru I learned about that morning
second hour geography class

rough diamonds
in the 1930's coat sleeve
lined in black taffeta

that night I dreamed
my bed was the shape of Peru
landlocked, yet water kept
seeping in, monsoon

the bubble of time
between moments
the planck numeral

In the middle of that night
under the table they almost
didn't find me

This is Hystra the trapdoor
Hystra the dice
in your unbroken life.

as if I'd disappeared
through a doorway
into now.

Thyr

The bar tab.
The phone bill those three months
you were in love with the flute player from Nepal.
The pounds of red grisly, granite-like cow stomach
you have actually consumed in the last year.
The packs of Camels, unfiltered, you have
palmed from friends:
"Just borrowing, no, I'm not smoking anymore."

The certain number of times only
you will see the moon rise, ringed moon,
blood moon, crescent, blackness.
Only so many heartbeats.
Only this many handfuls of daffodils for you
walking out on the hillside
hearing the song of a drunken man.

Clasping these many hands, shoulders, necks,
tracing these many thighs with your forefinger
like drawing the completed formula on a blackboard
this many kisses, sighs, comings and no more.

What can you do with a number like Thyr?
Do not turn it over to learn your final number.
Do not wade into thyr as you would an unplumbed river
        stirring pike teeth and stingrays and leeches.
Thyr is unwelcome at the campfire—the real ghost story.
Thyr is not to be laughed off.

Thyr is your hill, your daffodils and moons.
Thyr is your song.
You are the drunken man.

Lumaroon

The moon is moving away
from the earth
at a rate of one inch
per year.

You're losing rainforest
and topsoil and sanity . . .

The earth is losing its grip
of the moon's orbit like
a child its mother's hand.

But you're used to thinking
about that, you're not used
to losing the moon.

Like any mother moving away
from her child, the last orbit
wobbles, elliptical.

Just as you began to know
its lunacy and lore
the future moon leaves.

The mother dying
of cancer and the mother
dying of heart trouble

You will think the moon
a myth, her stories apocryphal.

ring the same space
prefigured as lunar trajectory.

Tidal waves and madness?
Nonsense.

That the child knows it will
leave its mother is fixed: a finite
point like a snapshot or period.

Huge ecumenical debates begin.
Nova produces a special.
The moon: Fantasy or Enduring Myth?

The next sentence
begins just anywhere
with a verb.

Phased out is the moon.

Some children divide their lives
into before their mother died
and after

In the end, a universal funeral
for dances and satellites.

believing then that
abandonment
can make a kind of sense

"What a strange
and lovely myth,"
you will say.

how death divides you
into two and also
leaves two holes

> *What will convince you*
> *is what always does:*

one in the ground
one in the sky

> *You will not be able*
> *to imagine*

What could have been.
What was not.

> *you would be given anything*
> *so beautiful.*

There was a woman who wore
her dead mother's shoes
everywhere

> *What convinces you*
> *is that you no*
> *longer imagine.*

In her head, she said:
"Here, mother, is the university
where you never went."

> *You will not be able to*
> *imagine you are worthy*
> *of such light*

Or whispers her name to candles
in the night club
her mother wouldn't enter.

spreading its silver weight
like opium on the diaphragm.

The shoes
were always
two sizes too large.

Why are you brought
to this moonless future

Some squeaked.
The heels clopped.

of less illumination

To the shoes she said:
Here is something
I could not fill.

more empty
than anti-matter?

But more often
the shoes against pavement
or soft moss

Because the moon
is only a little
walked upon

were the syllables
of her mother's voice.

and like doubting Thomases
you will put your fingers
into the wound
of the sky
lifting you higher than fear.

Leethum

It could go either way.
Six a.m. hits
like a Buick's tire squeal
and you find you haven't slept
and the blinking off streetlights
and even the dog is mad.

Leethum tallies the one more phone call
to the ex-spouse that reknits a bad marriage
like an orange/green afghan, or one more dialing
to the home shopping network, one more lottery ticket
which stands for whom you will eventually become.

Leethum tastes like sulphur and honey.
Leethum is a finalist:
a decimal point which banners your win
or a guillotine in the sentence beginning, "Almost."

Leethum is the janus number
the place where seconds extend
like two lifetimes:
a crossing guard or a traffic cop
looking both ways before you go.

Aegeranon

Land that looks like a sepia tint photograph
only needs some farm hand, *American*
Gothic with wooden
pitchfork

like a rustic Neptune, to stand before earth and
stars heralding the sweep of green-green
and azure of prairie sky
and flora

and spiky, tall grasses where all life is.
Each millimeter a nanosecond of teeming
each puddle where literally
invisible

heartbeats stir up the sand and the dragonflies
purple, black & white, scary orange
rule until a nuthatch or cardinal
with its blue

lace cracks them in two like a noonday
snack of perforated saltine. I'm glad
everything is tiny, save two
locust trees like

a long-married couple who link arms akimbo
trunks shadowed by the Serengeti tufts
of leaves where, behind, lie
what I think

are cottonwoods. Anyway, the leaves turn like fat
jade earrings in a multitude of ears shaking
and because of three firs, the height,
scale makes you think

of being on the bottom of a leagueless ocean
where sometimes, like today, the sunbeams
reach all the way through to the sediment
where humans,

those bottom feeders, live. No currents disturb
the continental shelf life here. Here, only
yellow tiger lilies hiding
among purple phlox,

wildflowers alien as blue anemones out on the prairie
where conifers look prehistoric, the first real
trees. Voices of the past flit by
like those yellow and brown-

winged insects I saw yesterday, couldn't identify.
Now bright flags, now their edge of wing is
a line in the air, thin as a gasp. It's like
the summer swoon of

a Tennessee or Alabama bride because it's so dreamy
or holographic to be able to look that far out
across verdant plants for a city dweller
circa late, late 20th century

as if it's not really supposed to be here, like how
you or I wouldn't be here, either, except
by an accident of birth and this
virgin prairie

unplowed through a couple entire centuries
unnoticed because unbelieved, like us,
too? Not supposed to have survived
the rush to land,

greed, loamy generations, crooked surveyors, cows,
accidents of development, disease, floods
that have been thwarted, fallen short
the mark of our own death,
thus far.

Xelah Xalong

For David Orlowski

The number of the Chinese fire horse
        the number of the names of gods
and what Pandora found
        in the box engraved on the emerald:
That which is too beautiful to be named.

If this is your number
        you have been saved from drowning
you have saved someone from fire
you were somehow not on the plane
        that crashed in Europe.
You carry this number inside yourself:
        It is not next.

You know who-done-it, that she
        is in Paraguay, how her partner
Will be caught.
If this is your number
        you smell like absinthe.
If this is your number
        the stranger at the bus stop asks you
if it is okay to embezzle
his wife's fortune and leave her
        and her lover for Aruba and forgiveness.
If this is your number you know whether or not
        to tell him she will follow.

You catch the quicksilver glimmer
        of the last Perseod meteor shower.
Stars wink open over your ceiling every night
        if this is your number:

You bear true witness
        the palms of your hands are diaries.

Cehu

akin to a Hopi word for feeling separate,
apart from others of your tribe.

What am I doing among the surgeons?
Their scalpels and starched lab coats
their sudden red ties—

a silk at which silk worms shudder.
This is my residency
on earth, weighing me down

like bedpan or cello
slipped between the legs
cold as performance anxiety.

I am the hopeful intern
I smile at the relatives
the soon-to-be-grieving wife

like a politician, like television.
Can I help it if I sketch
cartoons on status charts

mistake *rigormortis* for a pulse?
For heart attack, I write:
"sudden moment of clarity,"

for jaundice—a "golden glow."
When palpitations flutter like buttery tulips
I pen "Her left ventricle was all excitement."

As your life grinds down,
corroded Victrola, I'll record:
"His life ran away like a fox."

The pills I push are trochaic apothecary.
My tonics boast wine and tar.
These salves are beeswax, lavender, crushed glass.
They shine like pulsars in your lungs, like scars.

Callarum

This time when you cross over
the fieldstone bridge
the homeless man underneath
reaches up, beckons or waves
some hazy signal like a fogged lighthouse
and you notice the bluish glinting—
like a cloudy zircon facet
of your mother's engagement ring, now scratched
with dough kneading and the grinding of meat—
his left eye
the only good one
in the six a.m. sunbeam out
of a parting nimbus
like an ice floe into the mind
of fifty party-goers on the Titanic
that first, throat-tightening staticky anxiety.

You wonder, if you were walking
slowly, not driving, whether you would
give him coins, the Susan B.'s you've been hoarding.
Carried off like taliswomen
against some secret
you want to forget you know—
your mother's death? your child taken away?—
you wonder if he's beckoning
because someone else is there with him
underneath his granite canopy,
some human or pet obscured
as he asks for help or if the wave
was merely a reckoning
of your uninterrupted glaze, like a laser
over the heart of the highway.

And if he has waved or beckoned each time
before your blue Mercedes or six-pistoned Chevy
went barreling past, sure torpedo, but not past
the Andrea Doria doom
the water full of silly plankton
like this man, orange-earmuffed and fatigued
by Army surplus and circumstance
and he's just tired and pissed off
that you haven't exactly seen him
until this time, callarum—
like the instant you finally notice
a grasping, when your sister tells you she has
sold the zircon, broken down the setting
and settled for a pinkie circlet
darker, less worthy stone of topaz
the jeweler told her
would lighten in time and this is the time, callarum
that you are careful not to say the value of nothing.

Callarum is how many times you pass unnoticed
Yourself and how many times unnoticing.
Callarum is *until*.

Callarum comes for you
like an iceberg or a missile
like the man under the bridge
or the frame of the Hindenburg 16mm
replayed a callarum number of times
until you realize that
it's not the zeppelin singed like hair
not ring or bridge
but one man's disaster:
combustible, incendiary.

Zyster

> *"Yes, yes, the pyramids . . . but, after all,*
> *they didn't even have zero."*
> Overheard mathematics discussion

The cool thing
about Egypt
is that they had

no zeroes.
No teenagers feeling zilch.
No nada grandmothers.

No nil old men.
They taught
the mirror of functions

that subtraction
reflected addition.
I believe that's true.

For example, if you love
more than one person
this division

multiplies.
They taught this
at the same time

children learned
language using gold, silver
and brass bars

to hold in baby fingers.
This meant
their progeny

could not only say
what they meant but give
tangible examples of brass.

Of course, Nile dwellers also
threw away the brains
when they mummified

which is unfortunate.
They didn't think
the brain had any

important function.
"This funneled sponge?"
they said, "Pitch it!"

But the heart and liver
and spleen
they loved.

So, instead of
the emptiness, zero:
an ellipse through which

generations could easily fall
they had a place
for everyone already

like the spleens snug
in canopic jars,
hugging an alabaster pillow

and as if to say
"That's enough,"
or that you can't

hold your place if things
get too large
they stopped numbering

at a billion
for which the symbol
is a seated scribe

with arms stretching outwards
in astonishment:
"A billion!"

Kisura

As kids we always told the story
of Barbara Mullhall going down more
than three times at Myers Lake
and how her toes pointed
to the July sun like the mast
of an astrolabe, her body,
watery yacht below.
Then she rose like some bloated
undead, face red, heaving regular air.
First Kisura.

Kisura is the lazarus number:
deus ex machina, the cavalry,
breath in stone.
The dead one comes.
Kisura.

I've known it, too, saved when
I was seven by some older boy
my mother screamed at onshore:
"Jesus! She's drowning!"
And the two men I turned away
in the dark-finned Chevy
driver flicking his Camel
opening his door to me
like the lid of a navy coffin.
"Hey, little girl."
But I spun around
straight into a policeman
whom I didn't trust either, walked
all the long way home, eyes over
my shoulder, my head the antennae
cage on radar every half-block.
Childhood Kisura.

I was born in the perfect decade
of Jonas Salk and redemption.
Surely, that was Kisura.
Kisura says, "It just so happened . . ."

that the paramedics packed my blood type
when they came to get me
that when I slammed down hard
on linoleum slats
I heard my mother's voice
whisper in my head like a fugue.
Personal Kisura.

Kisura is the second parachute opening
The empty .45 chamber, the failsafe.
Coma heart and failed kidney pumping.
Second chance.
Take it.

Qualique

The other half of my life begins to answer the first
and it has this edge of *how come you didn't know that?*

like your first grade teacher snapping at you about
flashcards: 7 x 7 = 49!! How my mother always knew

her multiplication tables like how soon the mortgage
was due, how much her tips were, how much for

McDonald's french fries and the chocolate milkshake you
wanted but couldn't finish. What is thirst for? A famous

poet asked. I never told him that, at 17, I went around for
three weeks trying to answer the question he swung at us

like a baseball bat; it had something to do with *Playboy*
magazines and unquenchable things like power. I liked his

translations best. Little flashcard haikus. I understood spring.
But I still thought about thirst and its purpose besides biology.

What would you do without me? I asked my soon-to-be-husband.
Seriously? he said, *I would sit in this chair and never move.* Either

I scared or inspired him. There was movement. And why did a
certain editor keep writing, "I respect what you're doing," and

"Alas, not quite." I imagined him impervious to pain, his beach
house. Meanwhile, my mother said that power lines were giving

her headaches and possibly cancer. I discounted this
in favor of her two packs a day of L&Ms. And what did

she mean her life changed every seven years? Not the
intervals of her six marriages or the spacing of our four

births. I didn't want to be a sponge, absorbing
all this greatness. But then. First, a *New York Times*
headline: large concentrations of electric

power emissions are linked to health problems,
not only cancer and headaches. Also, the *Detroit*
Free Press reported that every seven years, all

the cells in your body are replaced (except brain
cells). Then. My husband began trips to Bogota
and Belfast, Ireland and many other places where

I didn't go but now I'm always the homesick
one and don't want to move. Entertaining a female

poet, I make the remark about the editor's perfect
life; she retorts "Oh, no, his wife ran around on him
and then got an enduring cancer and he had to take

care of her. His life is terrible." I wasn't glad to hear
this. Then another guy tells me it was even worse,

that the female poet was his lover and that's why
she defended him. But his wife did run around,
and that when he finally had his first affair with

the same female poet, the guilt was indescribable.
Plus, it didn't work out. Then my husband finally
answers directly, "I meant I would do nothing

without you," the perfect answer in his never-to-
be-published best seller, *The Husband Answer
Book*. And how come I didn't know that the lives

around me were a mirror of mine, although more
like a funhouse. The flashcards of inertia and desire

work themselves out by the stretching mirror, by
the kaleidoscope glass. What is thirst for? Will
you get up out of your chair forever?

Whirrol

Instinct, here, is a kind of insect love
as lethal as human love.
—John Patten, *Social Insects*, 1934

Admire the wasp's cinnabar
beauty, that hard-shell-
-in-sun appeal.

Donations of her voice floated
up to him

Even the rush of its wings
heightens senses

like strings of mica, galena.
He had to try strip mining.

like the unmistakable
sound of zippering.

Her jewelry gleamed
like dental instruments
selected chilly silver.

You wonder
whose clothes
are off

Her light brown eyes
sand on a shore
he trespassed once.

who will be stung
or liquefied
into honey—

Its cove of perfection
a quarter million
well spent.

crude amber
in the carburetor
of the hive.

She was from
the mesa
of doves

You want to say something
for the wasps
who left you alone

while he was
a lowlander
leathered by winds

after batting their bodies
against the few
screens that held.

from valleys
of tide pools
whetted by sharks.

They were helicopters
of politeness

The combustion was automatic
like a motor
or a rifle

that whizzed away
leaving octagon
hollows of wax

like how the magnetic field
rushes toward millenniums:
repel, repel, repel.

in the muscle
humans use
for a pump.

Infinity Money

I wish I had infinity money.
— Carrie Sturgeon, third grade

I sense somehow that it is blue, the sky of a summer's
day, the kind that starts at 6:30 a.m. with nothing

planned for the whitening diem. And your parents are
both alive and married to each other. And the other kids

on your block don't have it as good as you on your front
porch swing, looking up at the jade leaves of impossibly

tall elms, winking at you like there's some secret in
the swing's rhythm and your pilfered bedroom pillow

as you lie under the endless blueness of infinity money.
The writing must be a type of rune, hieroglyphic, or

sanskrit and read the same backwards as forward like
the snake that eats its own tail in the ocean of the world

or double-helix that is almost the dollar sign on the keys
of a typewriter. It buys ambrosia and everyone's life and

you cannot run out of it, no matter your trying. Its ink stains
your hands. You're a blue blood and I don't think you can

give it back. But they mean what the rich have. They mean
it like a kajillion, something they've never counted to but like

to say as a joke. They want nothing to stop, not Halloween
candy, love or bicycles. They are third graders. They mean

the new concept they've learned in class, one more thing they're
not supposed to know like sex or excess. That something goes

on and keeps going on makes sense. For them, more than
three is many and they have written this term in a wish. It's how

all the things they cannot pay for, yet will have to, are summed up
in this blue tender, how they know already what costs everything.

Philium

The telephone number you give the guy in the bar.
The age at which he first had sex he tells you.
The number of partners.
Your Aunt Florence's current age.
Any feasiblity study: philium.

Those missing in action in the official report.
Those deemed worthy of rescue.
The number of minutes to determine this.

When Abraham asked God to spare Sodom
if there were only a thousand good men
or only one hundred or ten
there was only a philium of good men.

Philium piles up like the inches of snow
your grandfather shoveled
at philium below philium—
increasing each time he tells you
and the number of times you tell
someone else he has told this story

like the leagues of lochness
and the length of its body
and the shadow of its head
and the body of evidence
level of radiation in milk
mercury level in mackerel
amount of lead in the Absopure
    mackerel

because one lead equals two babies
because three shadows mean six
    monsters
and two Geiger needles chart
    radiation
and prehistoric births tourist
    attraction
and three mothers file reports and
    two laws
beget more lawsuits and six lawyers
equals one settlement and three

toxins percentage in the river spawn regulations and
two fisheries spell
because one test means dead fish jobs and three
toxins means no monsters
because six dorsals means prehistoric double helix no jobs and no shadow means
no babies and one word means no river

when river and shadow and word
are one: philium.

Plancktion

The Planck numeral is a mathematical representation
of the shift of time in space, the distortions possible in a wave.
—Empires of Time

for Rodney Harder, artist

When Frank O'Hara talks about paintings by Bonnard
in his poem, *The Day Lady Died*, for Billie Holiday, you

are there and I am there already, even though it is 1959
and he has other things to do. That's because much later,

the *The New York Times* (the same one with her face
on it) will make another's breath come hard—

and you will tell me why O'Hara might have chosen
Bonnard, not Picasso to purchase, place in the poem.

The self-portraits, "unparalleled" says the *Times* reviewer,
also cause you to pause and look at distortions between

the red teapot, yellow heating register rendered in a kind
of dappled sun with faces like pinched wasps heading

for the yolky sugar jars. The self-portrait is a hollowed
out man with a theme of bipolar storms in his nucleus

eyes. He listens to a denser rhapsody there while
ordinary light shines like it's any day in a boring
life which makes this portrait infinitely abnormal but
familiar. You said on leaving, "I guess everyone's

a little crazy sometimes." How else could we turn our
faces from certain despair and work? Look how

the rusted teapot muscles the blue and yellow mosaic jars
like a losing prize fighter, how you explain space to me

how nothing is anything without being blown apart.
And this only a newspaper reproduction. I shudder, thinking

of standing before the real ones. And when you ask me
to New York, I almost think I'll go. For one half-hour

I see myself getting off a train long after O'Hara has
met his fate on Fire Island, after even Miss Stillwagon

has been married. It's how Bonnard's answer to cubism
is your answer to photographs. The things that break us

apart are responsible for something like these paintings
and the voice of Billie over decades. Any moment

I am looking at your canvas I am not thinking about
death. Hello. I am playing hopscotch and you are riding

a Schwinn and Frank is getting off at 34th and wanting
a shoe shine and he cannot imagine that the poem of this

day will be read to a million students who will imagine
their own streets beautiful now and Bonnard is thinking

of swirling a teapot red enough to overwhelm a yellow
heating register even though Picasso's friend and powerful

critic will not consider him worthy. And none of this
has happened. It is 1959, one Friday, in New York.

Randallia

I have been thinking of my mother's hand
all day, how the rise of its palm was translucent.
The hand is destiny, astrolabe and compass.

The hand that waved to me out of the blue
Buick, this morning, was her hand somehow
the child it belonged to a message.

How her palm skin was transparent
from kneading gluten, cupping men, my father
at what he thought was his root.

Their whiteness showing through to pink
capillaries, canals of thoughts I never
knew she had.

Their whiteness
like Bayer aspirin
if it were pressed into paper.

The heart's revolution wants
to overthrow the government of time, now
she's gone. How the world presses down

with its base ten digits, like an iron
pressing wrong a wrinkle where
none should be

or a fold in a newspaper and no one can say,
"Stop the presses!" in my life. I'm as flattened
as her skin pressing toward

that future I will not have
cut off from conversation, a glass
door never opened.

These last things I remember always:
how I never looked at her palmistry
how the lines there

might have foretold a fate more fortunate:
the left hand how to avoid
the destiny of the right

and was that the message
of the little boy, waving to me
out of the back seat

of the blue station wagon, trying
to tell me that besides his
own childhood happening

right now as he waved
his white palm at me like
the handkerchief flag of truce

rethinking my own childhood
whiteness of Bayer aspirin
onion skin lace of her hands

as she held me in her lap
as if the next game we played
would go on and on

when she put tissue paper white as bleached
cotton on two fingernails to fool me
when she said, "Fly away Jack."
"Fly away Jane." And they disappeared
and then, "Come back Jack,"
tissue reappearing

like a ghost, "Come back, Jane," emerging
like her hands, the way I remember
them shaking me awake.

The Number of Questions

Fortune telling machine
Great Lakes Metra Station, Illinois

1952 and the twin questions
of your weight and fortune
are somehow connected
in the glass of a four-foot high
vanilla ceramic and chrome
machine, where, for 10 cents
you may find solutions
small facts and dream
interpretation

Should I force the issue?
I dreamed of poison.
Which president had 14 children?

Standing in the decades old Metra station
next to the Navy men in doughboy white
creases with that square flap on their backs
like a spare flag of surrender:

Ought I?
I dreamed of manure.
What makes sunspots?

And the wooden everyman pews
ugliest shade of umber
and the Twilight Zone restrooms
where, probably, your doppelganger
waits to replace you.

Why does kindness affect me?
I dreamed of a manicure.
How many men were killed in WWII?

Everything you do not want to buy
is kept here: undercooked hotdogs, tacky
scarves, key chains inscribed with the wrong
spelling of your name.

I dreamed of love.
Should I indulge myself?
I dreamed of longing.

And so we read the questions
of some past we didn't know existed,
overly polite. We imagine their
undergarments were tricky.

Shall I dye my hair?
Did I do right last night?
I dreamed of medals.

Every crank of the quarter-sized knob
rolls forward yellowed queries
like vaulted papyrus.

Are my ideas sound?
I dreamed of kettles.
Whom can I dominate?

As if it were really that easy
all nightmares answered below
a thin, red line and you wonder
if these ever solved
anyone's life.

Shall I confide in a woman?
I dreamed of mad dogs.
What country has the highest mountain?

Plus those discrete nuts of fact
you take out in conversation
to crack someone open:

What is white coal?
Is the risk too great?
I dreamed of lips.

And we realize this is a real find
this mechanical ouija, the only object
worth anything in this junky commerce
and we want to know:

Am I attractive to others?
I dreamed of gloves.
Where do smiles come from?

And it will survive here, safe
like this moment of our twin histories.
The answer and questions read
their endless loop:

Will I travel?
I dreamed of pastry.
Am I lucky in love?

Here are all lost connections
of the world, titled, priced, captured
behind beveled typing:

I dreamed of kicking someone.
How many bones does the body have?
How shall I pay my debts?

So we keep scrolling far too long
like flipping through too many channels
or slowing down at an auto accident.

Should I tolerate selfishness?
I dreamed of prison.
What aquatic bird does not fly?

Because we notice the lever
of the trapdoor stencilled
YOUR ANSWER HERE
is stuck, like always.

I dreamed of kangaroos.
Am I being tricked?
Who held the first U.S. patent?

And this is so much
like the rest of my life with you,
the beauty of questions in a dingy place.
Tonight, we'll dream the answers
our kismet fate.

Will I meet my master?
I dreamed of laughing.
Where does the word comet *come from?*

photo by Lisa Powers

Josie Kearns was born in Flint, Michigan. Such journals as *The Georgia Review*, *Iowa Review*, *Poetry Northwest* and *Passages North* have published her poetry. Her first book, *Life After the Line*, (nonfiction), was published by Wayne State University Press. Her work has been anthologized in *Industrial Strength Poetry*, *Contemporary Michigan Poetry*, *Songs From Unsung Worlds*, *Passages North Anthology*, *Boomer Girls* and others. She has been awarded grants from the Michigan Council for the Arts and Cultural Affairs (now Artserve), the Cowden Fellowship, three Hopwood Awards from the Jules and Avery Hopwood Foundation, and the first MacLeod-Grobe Prize from *Poetry Northwest*. She has been a soda jerk, bank teller, reporter, factory worker, grants writer, editor, and currently teaches creative writing and literature at the University of Michigan.

New Issues Press Poetry Series

James Armstrong, *Monument in a Summer Hat*
Anthony Butts, *Fifth Season*
Gladys Cardiff, *A Bare Unpainted Table*
Lisa Fishman, *The Deep Heart's Core Is a Suitcase*
Edward Haworth Hoeppner, *Rain Through High Windows*
Josie Kearns, *New Numbers*
Lance Larsen, *Erasable Walls*
David Dodd Lee, *Downsides of Fish Culture*
Deanne Lundin, *The Ginseng Hunter's Notebook*
Joy Manesiotis, *They Sing to Her Bones*
David Marlatt, *A Hog Slaughtering Woman*
Paula McLain, *Less of Her*
Malena Mörling, *Ocean Avenue*
Julie Moulds, *The Woman With a Cubed Head*
Marsha de la O, *Black Hope*
C. Mikal Oness, *Water Becomes Bone*
Margaret Rabb, *Granite Dives*
Rebecca Reynolds, *Daughter of the Hangnail*
John Rybicki, *Traveling at High Speeds*
Diane Seuss-Brakeman, *It Blows You Hollow*
Marc Sheehan, *Greatest Hits*
Angela Sorby, *Distance Learning*
Russell Thorburn, *Approximate Desire*
Martin Walls, *Small Human Detail in Care of National Trust*
Patricia Jabbeh Wesley, *Before the Palm Could Bloom: Poems of Africa*